Science That's Appropriate <u>and</u> Doable

This science resource book was written with two goals in mind:

- to provide "good" science for your students
- to make it easy for you

What makes this book "good" science?

When you follow the step-by-step lessons in this book, you'll be using an instructional model that makes science education relevant to real life.

- Your students will be drawn in by interesting activities that encourage them to express what they already know about a concept.

- Your students will participate in hands-on discovery experiences and be guided to describe the experiences in their own words. Together, you'll record the experiences in both class and individual logbooks.

- You'll provide explanations and vocabulary that will help your students accurately explain what they have experienced.

- Your students will have opportunities to apply their new understandings to new situations.

What makes this book easy for you?

- The step-by-step activities are easy to understand and have illustrations where it's important.

- The resources you need are at your fingertips — record sheets; logbook forms; and other reproducibles such as minibooks, task cards, picture cards, and pages to make into overhead transparencies.

- Each science concept is presented in a self-contained section. You can decide to do the entire book or pick only those sections that enhance your own curriculum.

Using Logbooks as Learning Tools

Logbooks are valuable learning tools for several reasons:
- Logbooks give students an opportunity to put what they are learning into their own words.
- Putting ideas into words is an important step in internalizing new information. Whether spoken or written, this experience allows students to synthesize their thinking.
- Explaining and describing experiences help students make connections between several concepts and ideas.
- Logbook entries allow the teacher to catch misunderstandings right away and then reteach.
- Logbooks are a useful reference for students and a record of what has been learned.

Two Types of Logbooks

The Class Logbook

A class logbook is completed by the teacher and the class together. The teacher records student experiences and helps students make sense of their observations. The class logbook is a working document. You will return to it often for a review of what has been learned. As new information is acquired, make additions and corrections to the logbook.

Individual Science Logbooks

Individual students process their own understanding of investigations by writing their own responses in their own logbooks. Two types of logbook pages are provided in this unit.

1. Open-ended logbook pages:
   Pages 4 and 5 provide two choices of pages that can be used to respond to activities in the unit. At times you may wish students to write in their own logbooks and then share their ideas as the class logbook entry is made. After the class logbook has been completed, allow students to revise and add information to their own logbooks. At other times you may wish students to copy the class logbook entry into their own logbooks.

2. Specific logbook pages:
   You will find record forms or activity sheets following many activities that can be added to each student's logbook.

At the conclusion of the unit, reproduce a copy of the logbook cover on page 3 for each student. Students can then organize both types of pages and staple them with the cover.

SAVANNA

DESERT

PONDS

_____'s
Habitats Logbook

FOREST

POLAR

OCEAN

Habitats • EMC 859

Name _____

This is what I learned about habitats today:

Note: Reproduce this form for students to record science investigations.

Name ______________________________________

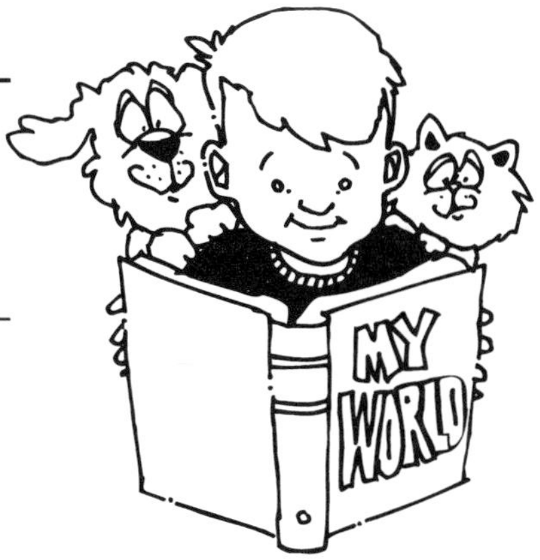

Investigation: ______________________________

What we did:

____

____

____

What we saw:

____

____

____

What we learned:

____

____

____

A habitat is a place where plants and animals naturally live.

Preparation

Before beginning the unit on habitats, plan learning opportunities for the students.

• Plan field trips to places such as an aquarium, a zoo, or a pond.

• Create a display of books about various habitats for students to use throughout the unit.

• Use your district audiovisual catalog to find appropriate videos and filmstrips to share with your students.

What Do Living Things Need?

Engage students in a discussion of what all living things need from their environment (*air [oxygen] to breathe, water to drink, food to eat, shelter for protection*).

Begin by asking students to explain how their own habitat provides each of these essentials for life. Record their ideas on the chalkboard.

Next observe a class pet (hamster, bird, fish). Ask students to describe what the animal needs and how it is being provided.

Explain that the place where living things get what they need is called a habitat.

When I need water to drink, I get it at a faucet in my kitchen. When our hamster needs food, we give him seeds to eat.

6

One Small Square

Read *Backyard* by Donald Silver (Learning Triangle Press, 1997) from the One Small Square series. Then have the students observe various small habitats around the schoolyard following these steps:

1. Divide the class into small groups. Give each student a clipboard holding a sheet of drawing paper and writing paper (see illustration).
2. Each group is to locate an area somewhere on the school grounds where there will be both plants and small animals to observe. They are to mark off an area to observe by drawing a 2-foot (60-cm) square in the dirt.
3. Students observe their square for a set period of time. They are to draw the living and non-living things and write about any changes they see *(A beetle crawled across the square. Some ants carried off a dead bug.)*.
4. Back in class, have each group share their pictures and describe what they saw in their small habitat. Compare the ways in which the habitats were the same and different.
5. Reproduce a copy of the logbook form on page 5 for each student. They are to record what they did, what they saw, and what they learned during the activity. Depending on student writing abilities, you may want each group to work together with adult help.

Kinds of Habitats

• Explain that there are large habitats (also called **biomes** or **ecosystems**) such as forests and small habitats such as a single tree. Brainstorm and list all of the habitats students know. Add to the list throughout the unit.

• Read books such as *Crinkleroot's Guide to Knowing Animal Habitats* by Jim Arnosky (Simon & Schuster Books for Young Readers, 1997) and *Richard Orr's Nature Cross-sections* by Moira Butterfield (Dorling Kindersley, 1995) to explore some of the different habitats on Earth.

• Reproduce page 9 for each student to complete.

Habitat Logbook

Begin a class habitat logbook. Ask students to recall what a habitat provides. Write this in the form of a definition on a chart entitled "A Habitat." The definition doesn't need to be complete at this time. Corrections and additions will be made as vocabulary and knowledge increases.

Have students copy the definition for their individual logbooks, using the logbook form on page 4.

A Habitat

A habitat is the place where a plant or animal gets the things it needs to live.

A Habitat Picture Dictionary

Begin a class picture dictionary of terms, places, plants, and animals introduced in this unit. You will need 27 sheets of tagboard and metal rings.

Use colored marking pens to make the cover on one page and write one letter of the alphabet at the top of each remaining page. Punch holes on the side of each chart for the rings.

Throughout the unit, select students to write terms and definitions on the correct pages and to tape in illustrations they have drawn and cut out.

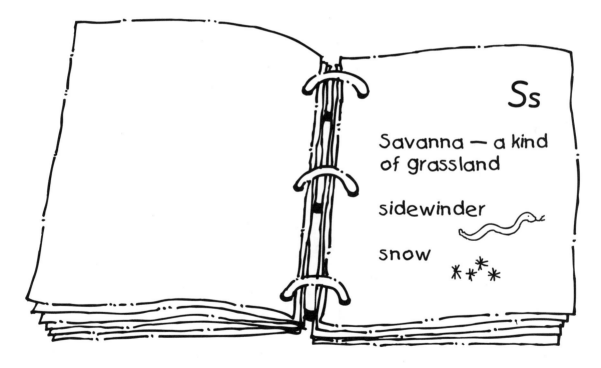

Ss

Savanna — a kind of grassland

sidewinder

snow

Refer to the picture dictionary when students ask about a term you have already covered. Students may use the dictionary when writing reports or original stories.

Habitats • EMC 859

Name _____

Find the Habitat

Circle the two water habitats.
Color the driest habitat.
Put an X on the coldest habitat.

A desert habitat has very little rainfall.

What Is a Desert?

- Make an overhead transparency of page 16.

  Ask students to tell you what they know about deserts. (Ask questions to elicit responses related to the weather, temperature, rainfall, and landscape of a desert.)

  Write their comments on a class logbook page entitled "Deserts." Write down all comments. You will make additions and corrections to the logbook at a later time. Show the transparency to help generate more information.

- Read books such as *Exploring Deserts* by Barbara Behm & Veronica Bonar (Gareth Stevens Publishing, 1994) and *The Hidden Life of the Desert* by Thomas Wenwant (Gareth Stevens Publishing, 1994), or watch a video about deserts.

  Discuss what students learned from the reading. Make additions or corrections to the class logbook page.

  Reproduce copies of the logbook form on page 4 for each student. Have them write about deserts for their individual logs.

A Desert Habitat

Deserts

Deserts are hot.

Deserts don't have much water.

Deserts have dirt and rocks.

Some deserts have big piles of sand.

         Habitats • EMC 859

Water Evaporation and Desert Life

Not only do deserts have little rainfall, most are very hot during the day. This means that water evaporates quickly. Use the following activity to explore this concept with your students.

Materials

- sponges
- container of water
- sidewalk or blacktop

Steps to Follow

1. Take students outside on a sunny day. Wipe a wet sponge across a section of sidewalk or blacktop. Have students watch as the water begins to dry up.

   Ask, "Where did the water go?" If no one can answer the question, explain that the water changed from liquid water to an invisible gas called water vapor and that the water vapor went into the air. Ask, "What helped the water to evaporate so quickly?" (the heat from the sun)

2. Give students wet sponges. Have them draw water "pictures" on the sidewalk or blacktop. Draw some pictures in the sun, some in a partially shaded area, and some in a completely shaded area. Ask, "Where did the water evaporate the quickest? The slowest?" Ask students to explain why this occurred.

3. Discuss how the quick evaporation rate in hot areas adds to the water problem in deserts. (The water evaporates from plants, animals, soil, puddles, etc., that are exposed to the air and sunlight.)

4. Explain to the students that they will be learning some of the ways desert plants and animals have developed to survive in this harsh habitat.

Habitats • EMC 859

Plant and animal life differs in the various types of deserts. The plants and animals presented in the following activities are found in North America's cactus deserts.

Desert Plants

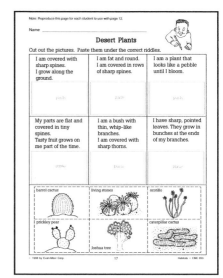

- Read about desert plants in books such as *Desert Life* by Barbara Taylor (Dorling Kindersley, Inc., 1992), *Cactus Desert* by Donald Silver (McGraw Hill, 1997), and *Discovering Deserts — Ranger Rick's NatureScope* (National Wildlife Federation, 1989).

Have students share what they learned about how desert plants have adapted to life in a place with little water.

- Reproduce page 17 for each student to complete and place in their individual logbooks.

Water Storage Investigation

This investigation models the way some cacti soak up and store water.

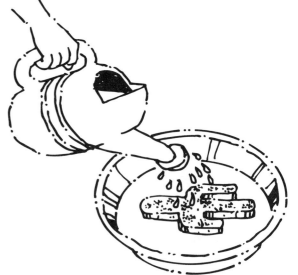

Materials

- watering can
- water
- dry sponges — one per group (The compressed ones available in many kitchen supply stores give a more dramatic result.)
- pie tins — one per group
- the form on page 18, reproduced for each student

Steps to Follow

1. Prepare the sponges by cutting them into cactus shapes with heavy-duty scissors.
2. Divide the class into groups. Give each group a pie tin and a sponge. Have students draw and write a description of the sponge on their record sheets.
3. Have each group sprinkle "rain" on their sponge "cactus" and observe what happens. Students complete the "Before" and "After" boxes of their record forms.

Follow Up

- Discuss how this relates to cacti in nature. (Many types of cacti have accordion-pleated surfaces. During rainy periods the pleats can expand as they store water inside.)

- Have the students complete the "What I learned" section of the record form.

Plant a Desert

Have students assist as you make a desert scene in a terrarium. (Or have students make individual desert gardens in shallow plastic bowls.)

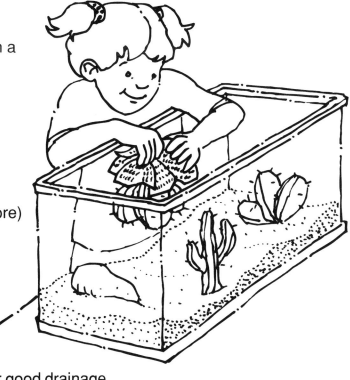

Materials

- terrarium
- several small cacti
- potting soil
- sand (purchased at a nursery or building supply store)
- fine gravel
- measuring cup
- spoon
- folded newspaper for handling cacti

Steps to Follow

1. Mix equal parts potting soil and sand.
2. Put a layer of gravel in the bottom of your dish for good drainage.
3. Spoon in the soil/sand mixture.
4. Make a hole for each cactus.
5. Put the cacti in the holes and gently press the soil around them to make it firm.
6. You can add pebbles, rocks, or other decorative objects on top of the soil. Optional — You may want to add a small lizard to live in your desert.

Caring for Your Desert

1. Water: Add a few tablespoons of water at the base of each cactus plant when the soil is quite dry.
2. Light: Most cacti will do well near a south-facing or west-facing window.
3. Resting Period: Cacti like a resting period during the winter. Move them to a cool room and water only about once a month.
4. Feeding: When your cacti are blooming, give them liquid tomato fertilizer once a month.

Desert Animals

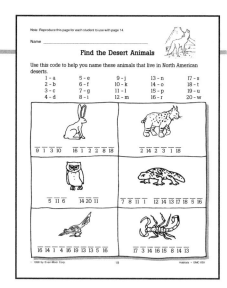

- Read about desert animals in book such as *Animals of the Desert* by Stephen Savage (Raintree Steck-Vaughn, 1997), or watch a video about North American desert animals.

  Ask students to recall what they learned about animal adaptations. Reproduce page 19 for each student to complete and place in their individual logbooks.

- Stay in the Shade — Have students take the roles of desert animals to explore one of the ways animals stay cool in the desert.

  Take the class outdoors on a hot, sunny day. Have them stand in direct sunlight and then in a shady spot. Ask students to describe the difference they felt. Explain that staying in the shade during the heat of the day is one way desert animals stay cool.

  Return to the classroom and discuss other ways desert animals stay cool (*Some come out only at night. Some have big ears to help get rid of body heat. Coyotes pant to help get rid of heat*).

- Read about life on a saguaro cactus from *Desert Giant — The World of the Saguaro Cactus* by Barbara Bash (Sierra Club Books, 1982).

  Discuss how the various animals use the cactus for food and shelter. Have students draw a saguaro cactus and some of the animals that use it as a home.

- Make any final additions or corrections to the "Deserts" class logbook page and to individual logbook pages.

Gather More Information

Reproduce the "Deserts" minibook on pages 20–24 for each student. Read the book together to review facts about deserts. Have students complete the pages.

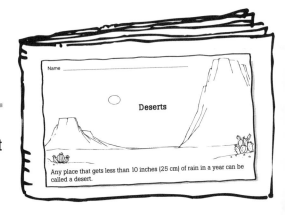

Make Desert Dioramas

Materials

- shoe box with one side cut out
- scissors
- paper and tagboard in different colors
- glue
- tempera paint and brushes
- sand
- small rocks, twigs, bits of broom straw
- modeling clay

Steps to Follow

1. Students use paint or paper to cover the back, sides, and bottom of the box. Cover the box bottom with a thin layer of glue and then sprinkle with sand.
2. Make plants to go in the diorama.
   Cut the plants from heavy paper or tagboard. To stand the plants, make tabs at the bottoms of the plants and glue them to the bottom of the box. Students might also use twigs for trees or they may model cacti from green clay. Add bits of broom straw for the spines.
3. Add animals made from paper or modeling clay.

> These same directions can be used to make dioramas for any of the habitats studied in this unit.

Summary Activity

Begin a class chart for comparing different habitats. Divide a large sheet of butcher paper as shown. Fill in the desert sections.

	desert	rainforest	pond	ocean	savanna	polar
describe the habitat				tide pools kelp forest open ocean		
name plants living there				tide pools kelp forest open ocean		
name animals living there				tide pools kelp forest open ocean		

A Desert Habitat

Habitats • EMC 859

Name _____

Desert Plants

Cut out the pictures. Paste them under the correct riddles.

I am covered with sharp spines. I grow along the ground.	I am fat and round. I am covered in rows of sharp spines.	I am a plant that looks like a pebble until I bloom.
paste	paste	paste
My parts are flat and covered in tiny spines. Tasty fruit grows on me part of the time.	I am a bush with thin, whip-like branches. I am covered with sharp thorns.	I have sharp, pointed leaves. They grow in bunches at the ends of my branches.
paste	paste	paste

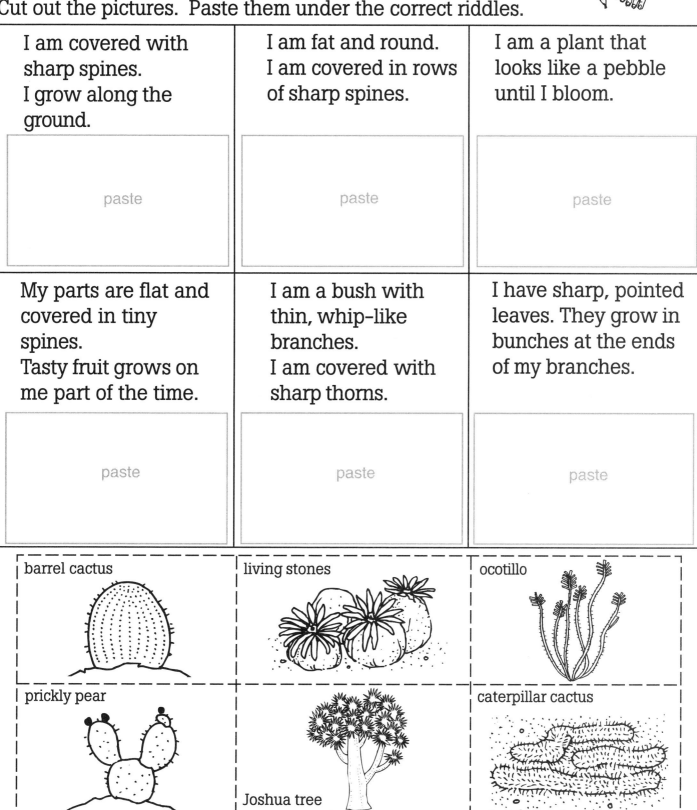

barrel cactus

living stones

ocotillo

prickly pear

Joshua tree

caterpillar cactus

Habitats • EMC 859

Name _____

Storing Water

Before

Draw the sponge.

Describe the sponge.

_____

_____

_____

After

Draw the sponge.

Describe the sponge.

_____

_____

_____

What I learned:

_____

_____

Note: Reproduce this page for each student to use with page 14.

Name _____

Find the Desert Animals

Use this code to help you name these animals that live in North American deserts.

1 – a	5 – e	9 – j	13 – n	17 – s
2 – b	6 – f	10 – k	14 – o	18 – t
3 – c	7 – g	11 – l	15 – p	19 – u
4 – d	8 – i	12 – m	16 – r	20 – w

$\overline{9}\ \overline{1}\ \overline{3}\ \overline{10}\qquad \overline{16}\ \overline{1}\ \overline{2}\ \overline{2}\ \overline{8}\ \overline{18}$

$\overline{2}\ \overline{14}\ \overline{2}\ \overline{3}\ \overline{1}\ \overline{18}$

$\overline{5}\ \overline{11}\ \overline{6}\qquad \overline{14}\ \overline{20}\ \overline{11}$

$\overline{7}\ \overline{8}\ \overline{11}\ \overline{1}\qquad \overline{12}\ \overline{14}\ \overline{13}\ \overline{17}\ \overline{18}\ \overline{5}\ \overline{16}$

$\overline{16}\ \overline{14}\ \overline{1}\ \overline{4}\ \overline{16}\ \overline{19}\ \overline{13}\ \overline{13}\ \overline{5}\ \overline{16}$

$\overline{17}\ \overline{3}\ \overline{14}\ \overline{16}\ \overline{15}\ \overline{8}\ \overline{14}\ \overline{13}$

Habitats • EMC 859

Name _____

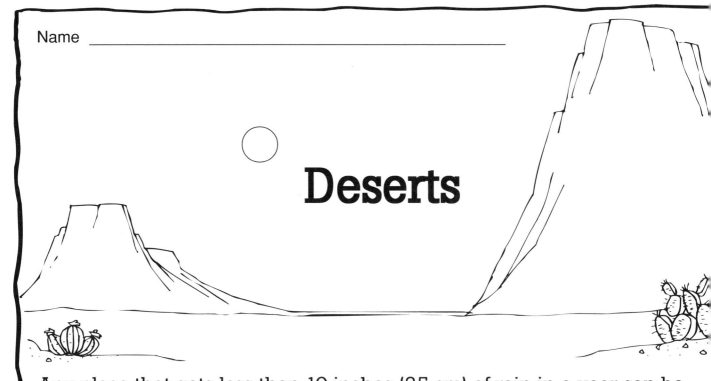

Deserts

Any place that gets less than 10 inches (25 cm) of rain in a year can be called a desert.

1

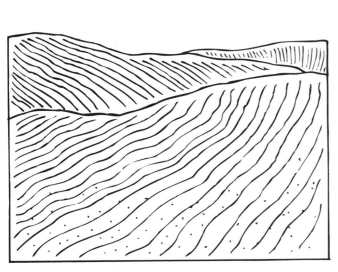

Some deserts are covered in sand. The wind blows the sand into mounds or hills called **dunes**.

Some deserts are covered with rocky cliffs and hills. Blowing winds carve the rocks into strange shapes.

2

Other deserts are flat, dry plains of soil and gravel.

There are even deserts that are cold.

But one thing is true about all deserts.
They get very little rainfall.

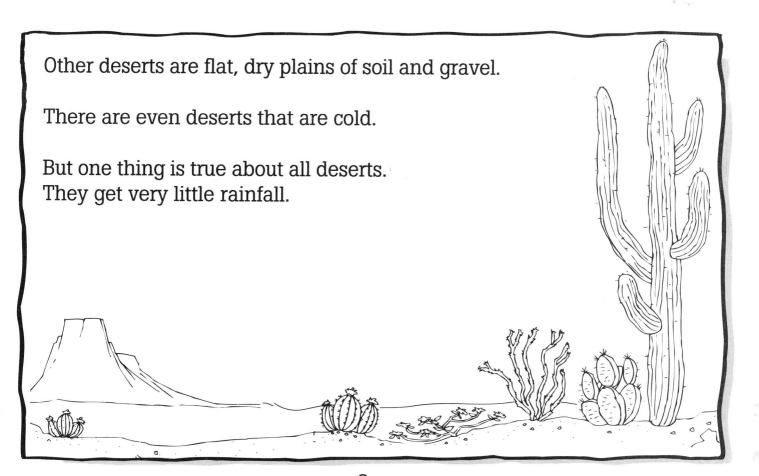

A desert seems empty because few plants grow there. The plants in a desert habitat must be able to live without much water.

In most deserts a lot of the rain goes back into the air **(evaporates)** quickly because of the heat. The desert can be very cold at night because there are no clouds to trap the heat.

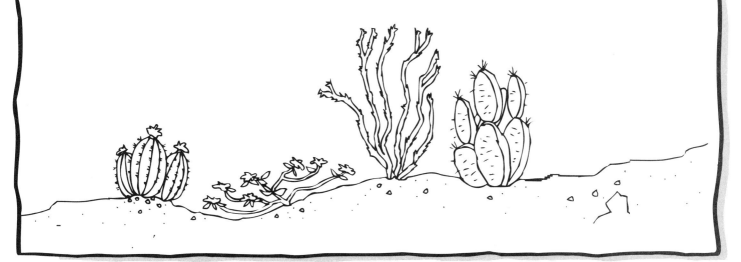

Desert plants have ways to live with only small amounts of water.

Cacti have thick stems that can store water when the rains come. Other desert plants store water in their stems and branches. They can live for many months without rain by using the water they have stored.

A lot of water escapes from a plant through its leaves. Desert plants have spines or small leaves to reduce water loss.

cholla cactus

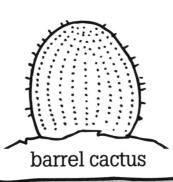

barrel cactus

ocotillo

The seeds of many desert plants don't sprout until there has been enough rain for them to sprout, grow, flower, and make new seeds quickly.

When a desert does get rain, it can become a colorful place filled with bright flowers.

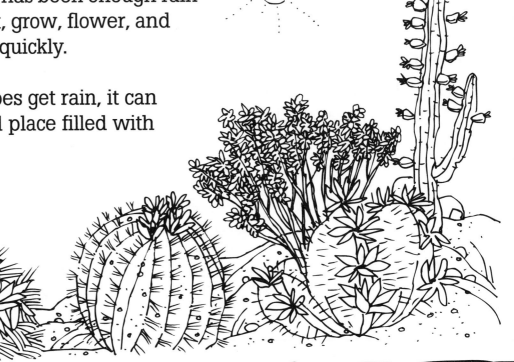

Different animals live in the deserts around the world, but they are all alike in one way. They are able to live in a place with very little water.

Many desert animals get enough water from the plants or seeds they eat. Some meat eaters **(predators)** get enough water from the animals they eat. Some animals get the water they need by licking the dew that collects on plants and rocks during the night.

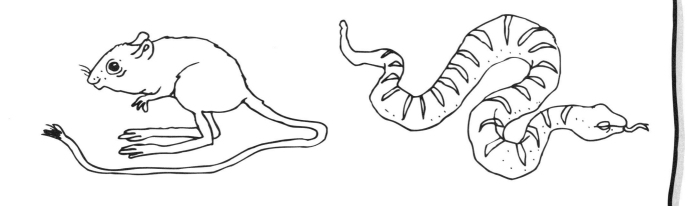

Heat is a problem for desert animals. Some animals rest in shady spots. Some live underground and only come out at night. Some are covered with hard scales that keep them from drying out in the hot sun.

9

When it does rain, tiny tadpoles, diving beetles, and desert shrimp appear in pools made by the rain. They must grow up and lay their eggs before the pool dries up. Some eggs are buried in mud. Others are wrapped in a sticky cover that gets hard when it dries. The eggs are safe until the next rainfall.

10

A forest is a tree-covered habitat.

What Makes a Forest?

- Make an overhead transparency of page 29.

  Ask students to tell what they already know about forests. (You may need to ask questions to help get them started.)

  Write their comments on a chart entitled "Forests." Explain that there are different kinds of forests depending on the amount of rainfall and the types of trees. Show the rainforest transparency to help generate more information.

- Read books such as *Exploring Forests* by Barbara Behm & Veronica Bonar (Gareth Stevens Publishing, 1991) and *Forest Life* by Barbara Taylor (Dorling Kindersley, 1993), or show a video about forests. Discuss what students learned from the reading. Make additions or corrections to the class logbook page.

  Have students write about forests for their individual logbooks using the form on page 4.

There are several types of forests—deciduous forests, coniferous forests, mixed forests—found around the world. The minibook on pages 35–38 describes several forest types. Because of space constraints, the forest activities in this section focus only on plants and animals in the rainforest. You may wish to develop your own activities for other types of forests.

Forests

Forests have a lot of trees.

Different kinds of trees grow in forests.

There are different kinds of forests.

Little animals and big animals live in forests.

A rainforest is one kind of forest.

Habitats • EMC 859

What Is a Rainforest?

- Read books such as *Nature's Green Umbrella: Tropical Rain Forests* by Gail Gibbons (Morrow Junior Books, 1994), *Rain Forest* by Robin Bernard (Scholastic, 1996) and *The Magic School Bus Explores the Rainforest* by Joanna Cole (Scholastic, 1997), and watch a video about rainforests. Discuss the characteristics that make a rainforest different from other types of forests (temperature is hot most of the time, plenty of rain, air feels moist and steamy [humid], lots of plant and animal life).

  Record information learned on a chart entitled "Rainforests" for the class logbook.

- If possible take a field trip to a zoo or aquarium that has a rainforest exhibit.

Rainforests

have lots of trees

have lots of other plants, too

get a lot of rain

are hot all the time

have many kinds of animals

Layers of a Rainforest

- Reproduce page 30 for each student. Read the page together, name the layers, and describe what is found living at each level. Discuss how each layer is like a small habitat with certain plants and animals living there.

- Reproduce pages 31–32 for each student to use to sequence the layers of the rainforest. Students are to name each layer and write about it. Students then cut the sections apart and paste them in the correct order on a sheet of 12" x 18" (30.5 x 45.5 cm) construction paper. Provide rainforest books for students wanting to obtain more information about each layer.

- Add a page entitled "Layers in the Rainforest" to the class logbook.

A Rainforest in a Bottle

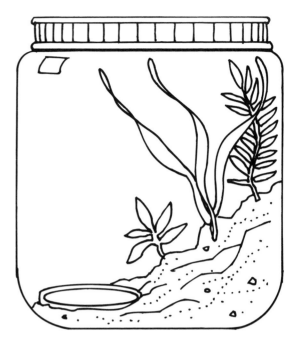

Have the students assist as you make a class "rainforest" in a glass terrarium or help the students make individual "rainforests" in large, clear, wide-mouthed plastic containers with lids.

Explain that a rainforest is enclosed much like a covered terrarium. In the rainforest, the canopy layer traps the heat and moisture, helping to make more "rain."

Materials

- large bottle with a wide mouth or a glass terrarium
- gravel
- sand
- peat moss
- small pan of water
- small plants: mosses, ferns, begonias, houseplants
- optional: small tree frog, turtle, or salamander

Steps to Follow

1. Mix equal amounts of gravel, sand, and peat moss for the soil of the terrarium. This will give you good drainage and allow air in the soil.
2. Put the soil in the terrarium. Make sure that the surface of the soil is at a slant (three or four inches thick at one end, slanting to the level of your pond [see step 3] at the other end).
3. Bury the pan of water at the low end. (This is the "pond" and will provide the basis for your water cycle.)
4. Put in the small plants.
5. Add a small animal if you wish.
6. Cover the top of the terrarium with a lid or piece of glass. (If you have added an animal, you must allow some air into the terrarium. Punch holes in the lid or adjust the glass to leave a small opening.) The water in the pond will provide enough moisture for the plants. The "rainforest" will need sunlight.

Feed the animal sparingly and remove uneaten food or it will decay. Frogs and salamanders will eat bits of chopped meat, earthworms, and flies. Turtles eat bits of hard-boiled egg, lettuce, berries, and commercial turtle food.

Rainforest Plants

- Read about rainforest plants in books such as *Inside the Amazing Amazon* by Don Leesem (Crown Publishers, 1995) and *Rainforest* by Betsey Cheesen (Scholastic, 1997). Ask students to recall the plants they learned about and to tell one interesting fact about each plant.

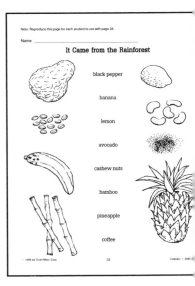

> *"Orchids don't have roots. They grow on other plants."*
> *"People use part of the kapok tree in life preservers."*
> *"Some of the plants we have in our houses came from the rainforest."*

- Reproduce page 33 for each student. This page lists some of the items we use that come from plants in the rainforest. Read the list together. Have students match the name of each item to its picture, and then circle any items they have used.

- Add a page entitled "Rainforest Plants" to the class logbook.

Rainforest Animals

- Read about rainforest animals in books such as *Animals of the Rain Forest* by Stephen Savage (Raintree Steck-Vaughn, 1997) and *Animals of the Rain Forest* illustrated by Debora Burr (Flying Frog Publishing, Inc., 1997), or watch animal videos. Ask students to recall the animals they learned about and to describe how the animal has adapted to life in a rainforest.

> *"A sloth has green stuff (algae) growing on its hair to help it hide in the trees."*
> *"Some frogs lay their eggs in the water trapped in plants."*
> *"Flying geckos glide from tree to tree."*

- Have each student select one animal to paint. Reproduce the report form on page 34 for each student to complete. Pin the completed paintings and reports on a bulletin board for everyone to enjoy.

- Add a page entitled "Rainforest Animals" to the class logbook.

Summary Activities

- Reproduce the "Forest" minibook on pages 35–38 for each student. Read the book together to review facts about forests.

- Make any additional corrections or additions to the class logbook page on forests. Have students write about forests for their individual logs, using copies of the logbook form on page 4.

- Complete the "Rainforest" section of the Habitats chart begun on page 15.

Rainforest Habitat

anteater   jaguar   boa   toucan   sloth

       Habitats • EMC 859

Layers of the Rainforest

Plants in the rainforest grow in layers. Each layer gets less light than the layer above it. Rainforest animals live in the layers where they can find food and shelter.

The **emergent layer** is the top layer of the rainforest. The tall trees reach up to the hot sunlight. Howler monkeys, harpy eagles, lizards, and spear-nosed bats live here.

The **canopy** has medium-sized trees. The thick green leaves make this a good home for animals. Three-toed sloths and silky anteaters crawl among the branches. Colorful birds nest and perch. Flying frogs and butterflies move from branch to branch.

Next comes the shady **understory**. It is filled with small trees and shrubs. Mosses, ferns, and orchids grow in the shady light. Tree frogs and snakes slither among the leaves. Jaguars hide in the trees.

The **forest floor** is dark. Here is where animals like the giant anteater look for food. Ants, termites, and beetles scurry through the leaf litter on the ground.

Habitats • EMC 859

This level of the rainforest is

called the _____.

It _____

_____

_____

_____

_____

This is the _____.

It _____

_____

_____

_____

_____

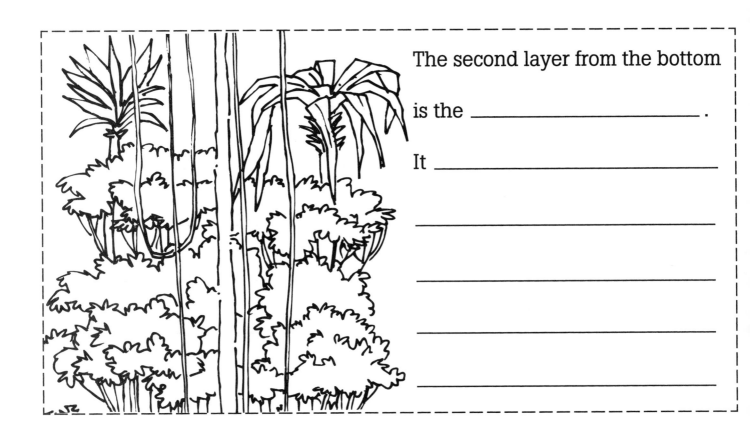

The second layer from the bottom

is the _____ .

It _____

_____

_____

_____

_____

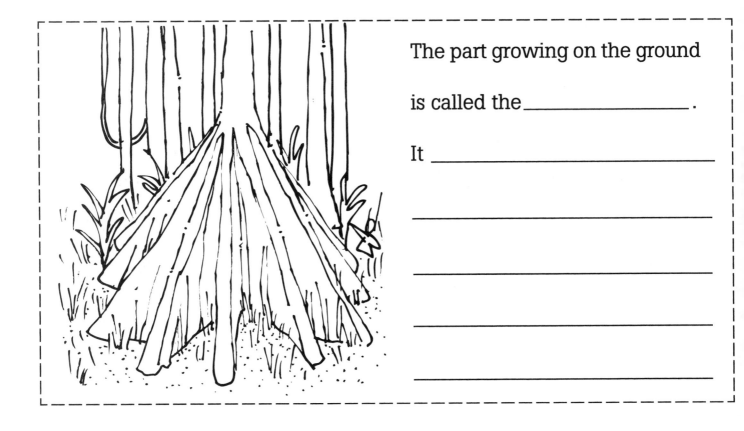

The part growing on the ground

is called the_____ .

It _____

_____

_____

_____

_____

Name _____

It Came from the Rainforest

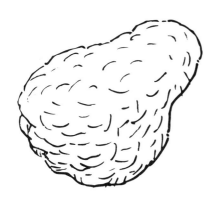

black pepper

banana

lemon

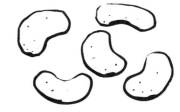

avocado

cashew nuts

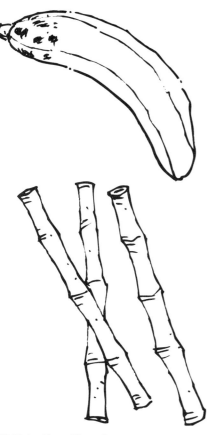

bamboo

pineapple

coffee

Habitats • EMC 859

Name _____

Rainforest Animal Report

My report is about _____ .
animal's name

My animal lives _____ .
layer of the rainforest

I learned these facts about my animal.

1. _____

_____

_____

2. _____

_____

_____

3. _____

_____

_____

Forests

A forest is a large piece of land covered with trees and bushes. It is made up of many kinds of plants and animals that depend on each other for food and shelter.

There are several types of forests. Each type has its own weather and its own kind of plants and animals.

Deciduous Forests

There are deciduous (duh-sij'-u-us) forests in many parts of the world.

In autumn the leaves turn many bright colors. By winter the trees have shed their leaves. In spring the trees begin to grow new leaves. By summer the trees are covered in green again.

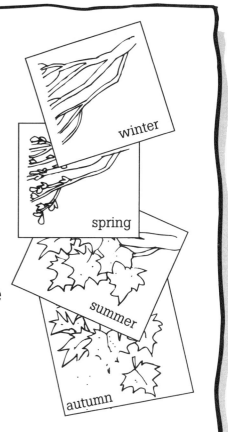

winter

spring

summer

autumn

Coniferous Forests

Coniferous (koh-nih'-fer-us) forests have evergreen trees. Conifers keep their needle-like leaves all year. The seeds of conifers are in their cones. The seeds fall out in warm weather.

Some conifers have thin, sharp leaves. Some have flat, rubbery leaves. Their cones are different sizes and shapes, too.

3

Almost all parts of a coniferous tree are eaten by some animal. The cones are filled with tasty seeds. The tree bark, buds, and needles are eaten as well.

4

Rainforests

Rainforests have tall, broad-leafed trees that grow close together. Most rainforest trees are evergreens—they keep their leaves. There is a thick tangle of other plants growing in and around the trees.

A rainforest is hot! There is so much water in the air that it feels sticky. The temperature doesn't change much from day to night or from month to month. In some parts of the rainforest it rains every day.

The plants in a rainforest grow so thick that they block out the sun. The ground under the trees is dark.

The plants seem to grow in layers. The **forest floor** is the bottom layer. Next comes the **understory**, then the **canopy**, which is like a big green umbrella. At the top is the **emergent layer** where the tallest trees reach for the sunshine.

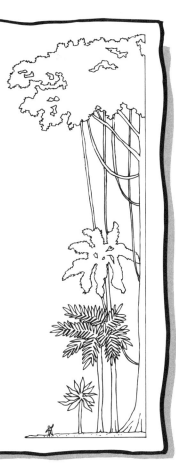

A rainforest is home to a huge number of animals, too. Animals live everywhere in a rainforest — on the ground, in bushes, in smaller trees, and at the tops of giant trees.

7

Circle the tree you would find in a coniferous forest. Put a line under the tree you would find in a rainforest. Put an X on the tree you would find in a deciduous forest.

8

A pond is a fresh-water habitat.

What Is a Fresh-Water Habitat?

- Prepare a fish bowl containing a small fish, a water snail, and small water plants. Have students observe this small habitat and describe what they see. Ask, "What kinds of animals are living in this habitat? What do the fish have that allows them to survive in a water habitat?" *(They have gills to breathe with. They have fins for swimming.)*

Explain that this is called a "fresh-water" habitat. That means the water is not salty like ocean water.

- Make an overhead transparency of page 42.

Explain to students that they will be learning about one type of fresh-water habitat — a pond. Ask students to tell what they already know about ponds. Write their comments on a logbook page entitled "Ponds." Show the transparency to help generate more information.

- Read books such as *Pond* by Donald Silver (McGraw-Hill, 1997), *Pond* by Paul Fleisher (Marshall Cavendish Corporation, 1998), and *Pond Life* by Barbara Taylor (Dorling Kindersley, Inc., 1997).

Have students recall what they learned from the readings, and make additions and corrections to the class logbook page.

Reproduce the form on page 4 for students. Have them write about ponds for their individual logbooks.

Note: Make an overhead transparency of this page to use with page 39.

A Pond Habitat

Ponds

Ponds are pools of water.

Some are large. Some are small.

Ponds have fresh, not salty, water.

Plants and animals live in the pond.

Plants and animals live around the pond.

Visit a Pond

Preparation

Plan a trip to a pond. Since you will be around water, recruit plenty of adult help. Have the students bring extra socks and wear play clothes and old shoes.

Materials

- long-handled scoop
- large white plastic bowls (2 per group)
- large sieve
- hand lenses
- clipboard and pencil for each child
  (See illustration below.)
- optional: video camera

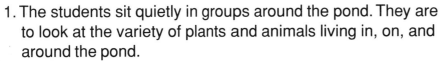

Steps to Follow

At the pond, divide the class into small groups to conduct each of the following activities. Students write and/or draw their observations.

1. The students sit quietly in groups around the pond. They are to look at the variety of plants and animals living in, on, and around the pond.
2. Fill one white bowl with pond water (try to have some living things in each scoop). Students examine the water using hand lenses to see what living things they can find.
3. Put a scoop of mud (strain it to remove most of the water) from the pond bottom in the second white bowl. Students are to separate any plants and animals from the mud and examine them with their hand lenses.
4. Optional: Have students assist as you make a video of the pond habitat to view in class. Include an overview of the pond as well as close-ups of the different types of animals and plants living there.

hole with string for pencil

cardboard

paper stapled to cardboard

Follow Up

Back in class, have the students describe the pond and tell about the plants and animals they saw living in and around it. Have the students use their notes from the trip to write about the pond for their individual logbooks, using the form on page 4.

Investigate Surface Tension

- Have students recall the plants and animals they saw on the surface of the pond. Ask them to explain how the insects were able to walk on the water without sinking. Use the following demonstration to help students see surface tension:

1. Divide the class into partners. Have each pair fill a glass with water right up to the brim. The teacher moves from group to group, adding a bit more water until students can see the curve of the water above the container.

2. Give each pair a piece of broom straw. Have one person gently drop the broom straw onto the water's surface. (Demonstrate how to hold the straw just above and perpendicular to the water before letting go of it.)

Explain that insects that walk on the surface of ponds are supported by the water's "skin." The skin bends a little around their feet, just like it does around the broom straw; but because the insect is so light, the surface skin does not give way.

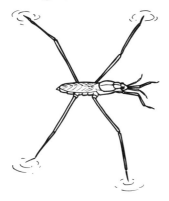

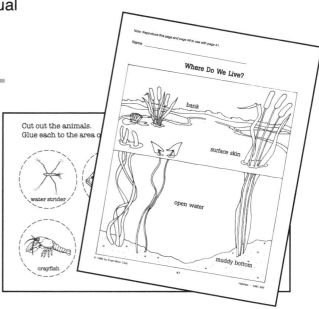

- Have students record the investigation for their individual logbooks, using the form on page 5.

Summary Activities

- Reproduce the "Fresh-Water Habitats" minibook on pages 43–46 for each student. Read and discuss the book together. Have students complete the pages.

- Reproduce pages 47 and 48 for each student. Review where the different animals are found in the pond. Students cut out and paste the plants and animals on the pond form.

- Complete the "Pond" section of the Habitats chart begun on page 15.

Note: Make an overhead transparency of this page to use with page 39.

A Pond Habitat

Name _____

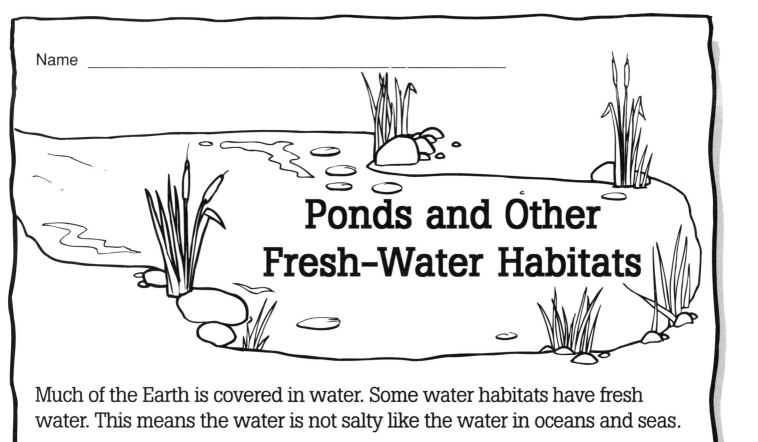

Ponds and Other Fresh-Water Habitats

Much of the Earth is covered in water. Some water habitats have fresh water. This means the water is not salty like the water in oceans and seas.

1

Most rivers, lakes, and ponds have fresh water. Freshwater habitats around the world are the same in some ways. There are plants that live in the water or along the shore. There are fish of some kind. There are likely to be snails, frogs, and water snakes. And there are birds and mammals that like to live near water.

stonewort

duck

duckweed

catfish

cattail

frog

2

A pond has many different kinds of plants and animals living in or near it. Some of the animals live in the pond all of the time.

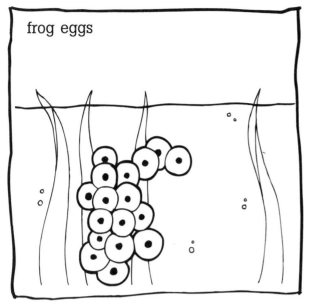

frog eggs

Some lay their eggs in the water.

Some find food in the pond.

3

Some animals live on the surface of the pond.

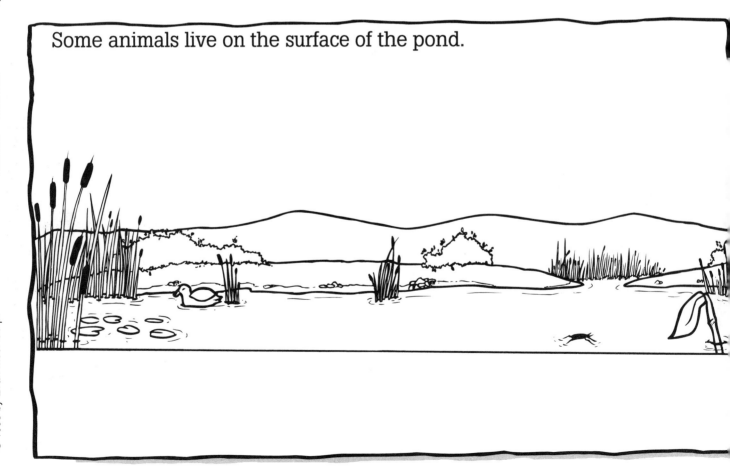

4

Some animals live in the open water.

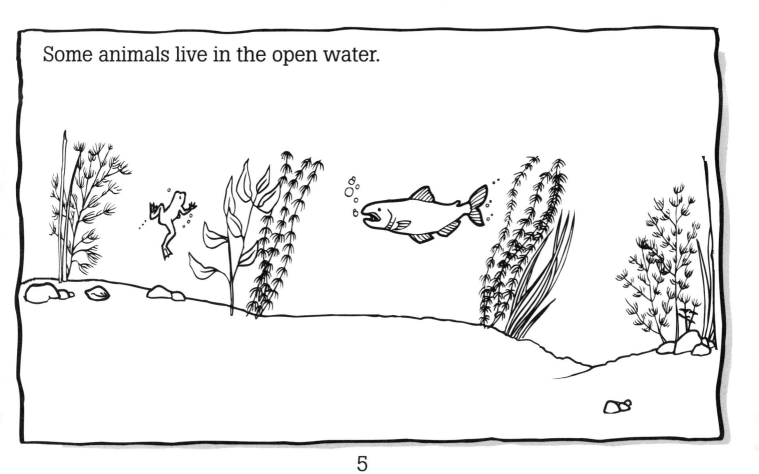

Some animals live in the mud at the bottom of the pond.

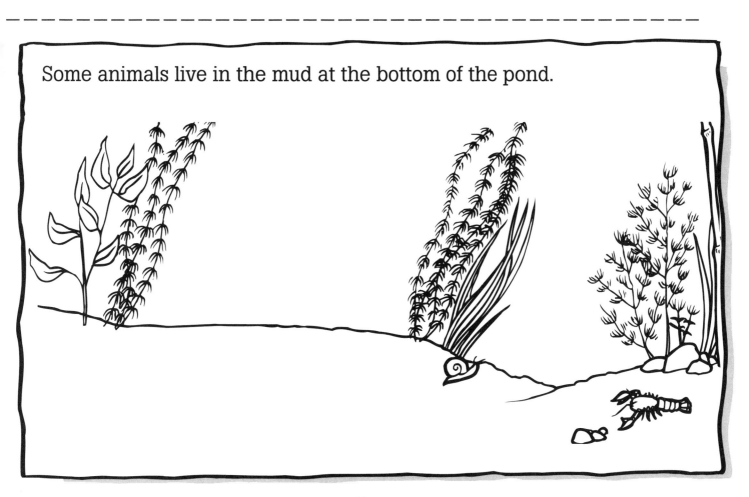

Larger animals that live on land come to the pond to eat insects, fish, and plants that live in the water. Some birds build nests along the pond.

7

- -

Water plants make food and oxygen (ok'–sih–juhn) for the animals living there. The plants can be a home or a hiding place, too. Some animals lay their eggs on the plants.

horsetail

arum

cattail

water lilies

pondweed

elodea

fanwort

8

Note: Reproduce this page and page 48 to use with page 41.

Name _____

Where Do We Live?

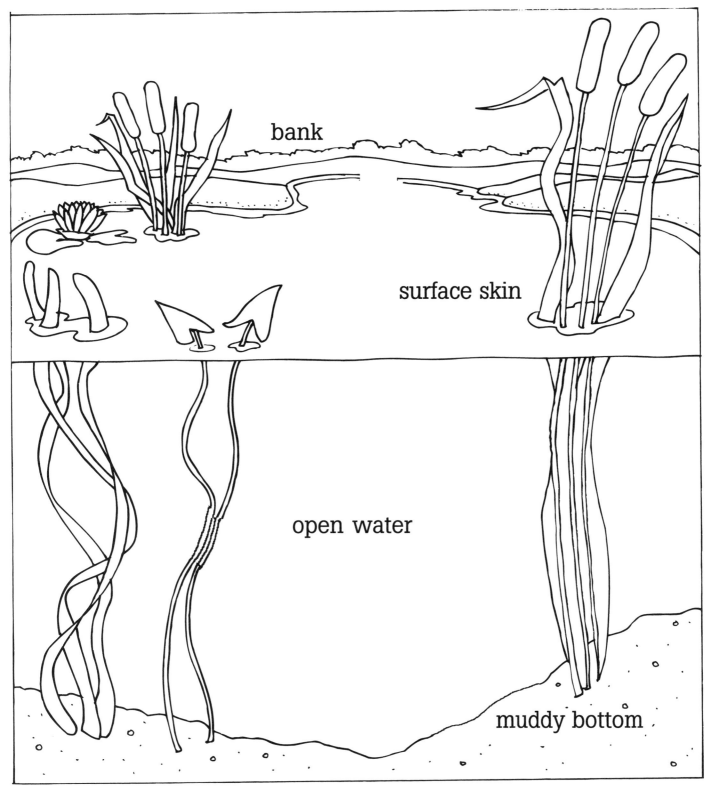

bank

surface skin

open water

muddy bottom

Habitats • EMC 859

Cut out the animals.

Glue each to the area of the pond where it would be found.

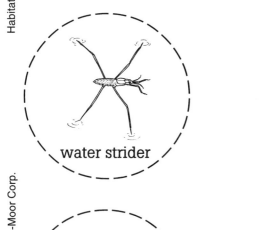

water strider

sunfish

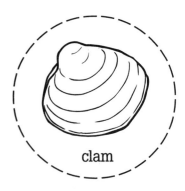

clam

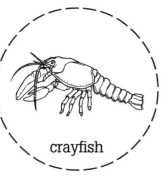

crayfish

raccoon

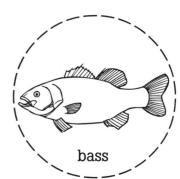

bass

Cut out the animals.

Glue each to the area of the pond where it would be found.

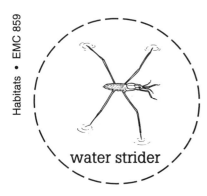

water strider

sunfish

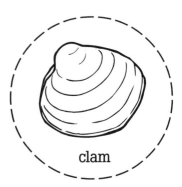

clam

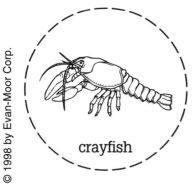

crayfish

raccoon

bass

An ocean is a salt-water habitat.

A Salt-Water Habitat

• Make an overhead transparency of page 54.

Explain to students that they are going to be learning about a salt-water habitats — tide pools, kelp forest, and open ocean. Ask students to tell what they already know about oceans. (You may need to ask questions to help get them started.)

Write their comments on a logbook page entitled "Oceans." Show the transparency to generate more information.

• Read books such as *Ocean* by Miranda MacQuitty (Knopf, 1995) and *The Magic School Bus on the Ocean Floor* by Joanna Cole (Scholastic, 1992), or show a video about oceans.

Discuss what students learned from the reading. Make additions or corrections to the class logbook page.

Have students write about oceans for their individual logbooks, using the form on page 4.

Fresh Water or Salt Water?

In learning about ponds and oceans, students have heard the terms "fresh water" and "salt water." The following demonstration will give students a concrete understanding of what salt water is.

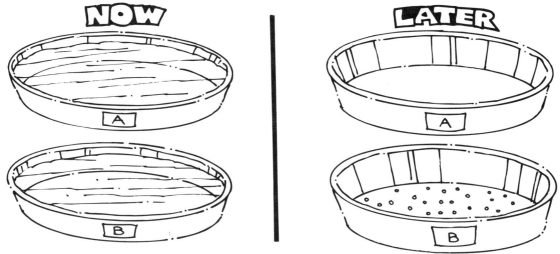

Materials

- shallow container of fresh water labeled A
- shallow container of salt water labeled B (make a solution of one part salt to eight parts water)
- logbook form on page 5, reproduced for each student

Steps to Follow

1. Show the two containers of water. Have students observe the liquids to see if they can tell which is which. (The liquids will look the same since the salt has dissolved into the water.)
2. Place the containers in a sunny location.
3. Students complete the "what we did" section of the logbook form.
4. Retrieve the containers when all the water has evaporated and observe what has happened.
5. Help students draw conclusions about what they have seen by asking questions such as these:
   "What do you see in bowl A? In bowl B?"
   "Which water sample was salt water? How do you know?"
   "Which water sample could have come from a pond? Why?"
   "Which water sample could have come from an ocean? Why?"
6. Students complete their record forms, telling what they saw and what they learned.

Ocean Plants and Animals

An ocean is a vast area consisting of many different habitats with one thing in common—salty water. The activities that follow help students explore three ocean habitats: tide pools, kelp forest, and open ocean.

                                       Habitats • EMC 859

- Share books such as *Life in a Tide Pool* by Allan Fowler (Children's Press, 1996). Ask students to recall the types of plants and animals living in a tide pool.

- Write a page entitled "Tide Pools" for the class logbook.

- Reproduce page 55 for each student. They are to circle the animals living in the tide pool.

- Have students write about tide pools, using copies of the logbook form on page 4.

- If possible, visit a tide pool for a close look at the plants and animals. If not, visit a pet shop that has salt-water aquariums set up.

Tide Pools

Tide pools are along the shore.

The water moves in and out.

Plants called algae live on the rocks.

Small animals live in the tide pool.

Kelp Forest

- Share appropriate parts of books such as *Beneath the Waves: Explore the Hidden World of the Kelp Forest* photographed by Norbert Wu (Chronicle Books, 1997) and *Kelp Forest* by Judith Conner and Charles Baxter (Monterey Bay Aquarium Foundation, 1989). Ask students to recall facts about giant kelp and the animals living in it.

- Write a page entitled "Kelp Forest" for the class logbook.

- Reproduce page 56 for each student. Read the information together and then have students cut out the animals and paste them in the kelp forest.

- Have students write about kelp forests, using copies of the logbook form on page 4.

Kelp Forest

Giant kelp grows in the ocean.

It is very tall.

Fish swim in the kelp.

Otters wrap up in it.

Starfish and crabs crawl around the bottom of the kelp.

- Read books such as *The Ocean* by Mel Higginson (Rourke Corporation, 1994), *Animals of the Oceans* by Stephen Savage (Raintree Steck-Vaughn, 1997), and *Sea Searcher's Handbook: Activities from the Monterey Bay Aquarium* by Pam Armstrong (Roberts Rinehart Publishers, 1996), and show videos about the open ocean.

- Write a page entitled "Open Ocean" for the class logbook.

- Reproduce page 57 for each students. They are to color the animals that belong in the open ocean and cross out the animals that don't.

- Have students write about the open ocean, using copies of the logbook form on page 4.

- Visit an aquarium if you have one nearby. Write about the trip using the logbook form on page 4.

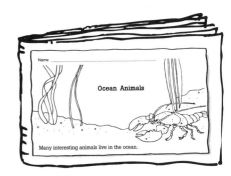

Note: Reproduce this page for students to use with page 52.

Name _____

What Belongs in the Open Ocean?

Color the animals that belong in the open ocean.
Put an X on the animals that do not belong.

Open Ocean

The ocean is big.

It is very deep, too.

Whales swim in the ocean.

Jellyfish float in the ocean.

Many kinds of fish live in the ocean.

Summary Activities

- Reproduce the minibook on pages 58–61 for each student. Read and discuss the book together to review the various types of animals living in the ocean habitats.

- Complete the "Ocean" section of the Habitats chart begun on page 15.

Name _____

Ocean Animals

Many interesting animals live in the ocean.

Extension Activity — Our Ocean ABC Book

Make a class alphabet book of ocean plants and animals. Have a selection of books about sea life available for student reference as they make their selections and illustrations.

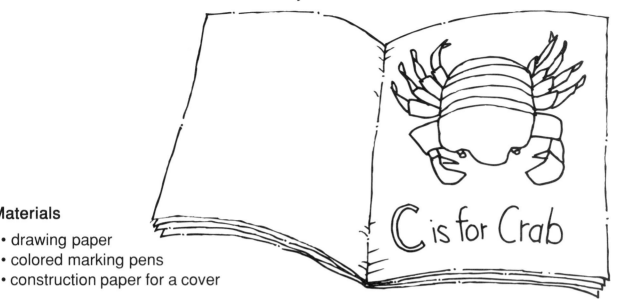

Materials

- drawing paper
- colored marking pens
- construction paper for a cover

Steps to Follow

1. Brainstorm to create a list of ocean plants and animals that can be used in the book. Write these on the chalkboard.
2. Assign one letter to each student in class. Have students illustrate and label their plant or animal on the drawing paper using marking pens.
3. Select someone to illustrate a cover for the book.
4. Arrange the pages in alphabetical order. Staple them together in the cover. Cover the staples with book binding tape.

Use ideas from this list to help you fill in the letters on your class list. You may want to give a prize to any student coming up with an "x" suggestion.

a—anemone, angelfish, algae, albatross
b—barnacle, barracuda, butterfly fish, bristle worm
c—cockle, crab, cuttlefish, cormorant, chiton
d—dolphin, dogfish
e—eel, eagle ray
f—fanworm, feather boa kelp, file fish, flying fish
g—goby, gar, goosefish, guitarfish
h—hermit crab, hagfish, halibut, hydroid, hawkbill turtle
i—Ida's miter
j—jellyfish
k—kelp, king crab
l—limpet, lobster, lamprey, lungfish
m—mussel, mackerel, moonsnail, moray eel

n—nudibranch, nurse shark, northern puffer
o—oyster, octopus, orca
p—pelican, prawn, puffin, periwinkle, porpoise
q—queen conch, quahog, queen angelfish
r—ray, rose star, redfish, roughie
s—sand dollar, squid, shark, sea star, seahorse
t—turban snail, tubeworm, triggerfish, tuna
u—urchin, urn sponge, unicornfish
v—viperfish, vase sponge, velvet fish
w—white shark, whale, walrus, wrasse, wolf herring
x—?
y—yellowfin tuna, yellow anemone
z—zooplankton

Note: Alphabet books can be made for any of the habitats studied in this unit

 Habitats • EMC 859

Note: Make an overhead transparency of this page to use with page 49.

Ocean Habitats

Habitats • EMC 859

Name _____

Tide Pool

Circle the animals living in this tide pool.

Habitats • EMC 859

Name _____

Giant Kelp—An Ocean Forest

Kelp is a name for a group of large seaweeds that sometimes grow over 100 feet tall. There are three parts to a kelp plant:

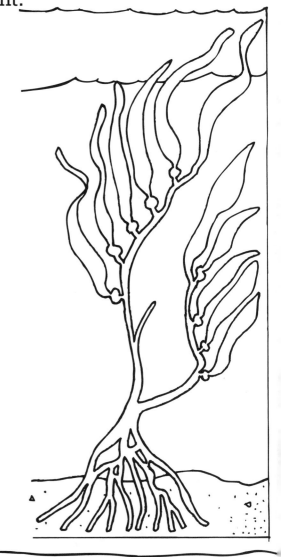

Holdfast — It looks like a root, but it just holds the kelp to a rock so it won't be swept away by the tide. Small sea animals like crabs, snails, brittle stars, and worms live here.

Stipe — The stipe is like a stem. It is tough, but it bends easily. Food moves through the stipe to the bottom of the kelp. Sea snails move up and down the stipes. Many fishes swim here.

Blade — The blade looks like a leaf. It makes food for the kelp plant. It makes spores which produce new kelp plants. Hollow bumps filled with air (floats) pull the blades up to the surface where they can get more sunlight. Sea otters swim here. The otters wrap up in the kelp when they sleep so they won't float too far from shore.

Cut out and paste the pictures on the kelp plant.

  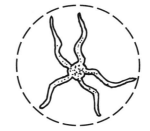 

Habitats • EMC 859

Name _____

What Belongs in the Open Ocean?

Color the animals that belong in the open ocean.
Put an X on the animals that do not belong.

Habitats • EMC 859

Name _____

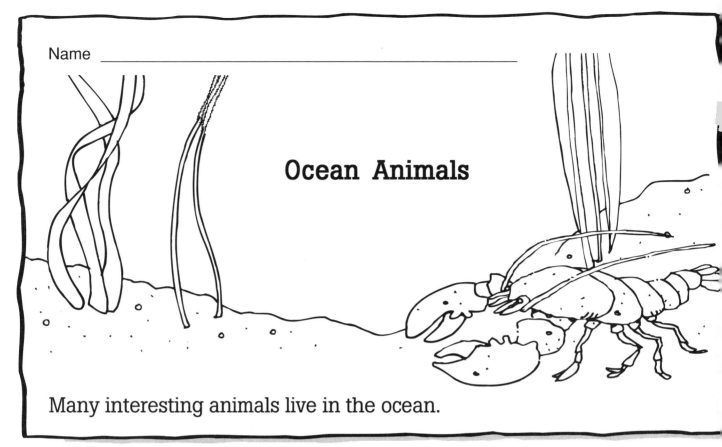

Ocean Animals

Many interesting animals live in the ocean.

1

Ocean animals have adapted (uh-dap'-ted) to be able to live in salty water.

Some live in places where tides move in and out.

Others live far from land in the open ocean.

2

Many of the animals that live in the ocean do not have a backbone.

These animals have hard shells.

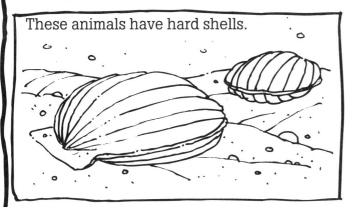

These animals wear their skeletons on the outside.

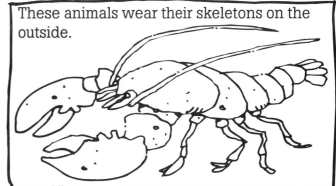

The octopus has a soft body and no skeleton or shell at all.

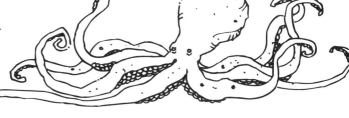

Thousands of different kinds of fish live in the ocean. Fish come in many colors, shapes, and sizes.

Fish live near the shore. They live in the open ocean. Some even live on the bottom of the sea.

Fish breathe with gills. Most fish are covered in scales and use fins to swim.

The seahorse lives near the shore.

The salmon lives in the open sea.

There are two big groups of fish.

Some fish have a skeleton of bone.

Some fish have a skeleton of cartilage (kar–tl–ij).

5

Mammals on land breathe with lungs. Mammals in the ocean breathe with lungs, too. They can stay under water for a long time, but they must still come to the surface to breathe.

Some ocean mammals live near land. They may crawl out of the water part of the day. Some ocean mammals swim far out in the ocean.

dolphin

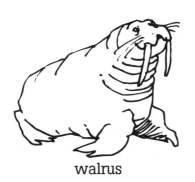

walrus

whale

6

Have you ever spent a day at the beach watching the birds? They fly out over the water. Some dive down into the ocean to catch food. Some rest on the rocks. Others run up and down the sandy beach.

gull

pelican

Most water birds have oily feathers and a layer of fat to keep them warm and dry.

Draw a bird on the beach.
Draw a star fish near the shore.
Draw a fish swimming in the kelp.
Draw a whale swimming in the open ocean.

A savanna is a grassland habitat.

Grasslands

- Make an overhead transparency of page 64.

- Read books such as *Grasslands* by Rose Pipes (Raintree Steck-Vaughn, 1998) and *Prairie* by Dorothy Henshaw Patent (Holiday House, 1996) to introduce the concept of grasslands. Ask students to describe a grassland and recall animals that live on grasslands.

Savanna

Explain to students that they are going to be learning about one special kind of grassland — the savanna in Africa.

- Read books such as *African Savanna* by Donald Silver (Learning Triangle Press, 1997), the savanna section of *Grasslands — Nature Search* by Andrew Langley (Reader's Digest Association, Inc., 1993), or show a video about the African savanna. Discuss what students learned from the reading. Begin a class log page entitled "Savanna."

Plants of the Savanna

Reproduce page 65 for each student. Read and discuss the page together. Have students complete the page to show what they recall about savanna plants.

Savanna

A savanna is a kind of grassland in Africa.

The savanna is hot.

Grass and a few trees and bushes grow there.

Herds of animals eat the grass.

Habitats • EMC 859

Animals of the Savanna

- Read the parts of *African Animals* by Caroline Arnold (Morrow, 1997) that relate to animals living on the savanna. Ask students to recall the names of the animals. List these on the chalkboard.

- Reproduce the form on page 66 for each student. Have students select one animal from the class list to draw and write a riddle about.

  Pin the riddles to a bulletin board entitled "What Am I?"

- If you have a zoo in your area, plan a field trip. Write a record of the field trip for the class logbook. Have students write about their experiences at the zoo using the logbook form on page 4.

Savanna Seasons

Many parts of the world have four seasons based on the weather. On the savanna there are two seasons based on rainfall — the dry season and the rainy season. Use the following activity to demonstrate the two seasons and to help students understand the effect on the plant and animal life.

1. Plant two dish gardens using identical plants. Place a jar lid in each garden to be a watering hole. Label one garden "rainy season" and the other "dry season."
2. Each day for two weeks, water the rainy season garden but not the dry season garden.
3. At the end of two weeks, have students examine the two gardens and describe what they see *(The rainy season garden is green and there is water in the pool. The dry season garden has dead plants and no water.)*. Ask students to think about how this affects animals living on the savanna. *(In the dry season, there wouldn't be much food or water.)*

Summary Activities

- Reproduce the "Grasslands" minibook on pages 67–69 to review the savanna and to learn about some of the grasslands of North and South America.

- Complete the "Savanna" section of the Habitats chart begun on page 15.

- Make additions or corrections to the "Savanna" page of the class logbook. Use copies of page 4 for students to write about the savanna for their individual logbooks.

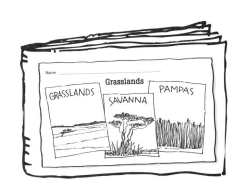

Note: Make an overhead transparency of this page to use with page 62.

A Grassland Habitat

Name _____

Plants on the Savanna

Grasslands have been on Earth for millions of years. The grasslands in Africa are called the savanna. The savanna is covered in grasses with a few tall trees scattered around.

Grasses have long, thin leaves. Their flowers grow all bunched up at the tips of long, round stems.

There are different kinds of grasses growing on the savanna. Some are so tall animals can hide among the them. Others are short. Some of the grasses (**perennials**) live for many years. Other grasses (**annuals**) grow new from seeds every year.

Elephants and giraffes eat the leaves and twigs of the trees. Herd animals like zebras and gazelles eat the grasses.

Match:

1. African grasslands are called   grow on the savanna.

2. Grasses have   eat tree leaves and twigs.

3. A few tall trees   the savanna.

4. Herd animals   long, thin leaves.

5. Elephants and giraffes   for millions of years.

6. Grasslands have been on Earth   among the tall grasses.

7. Some animals hide   eat the grasses.

 Habitats • EMC 859

fold

Name _____

_____

_____

_____

_____

_____

What Am I?

Grasslands

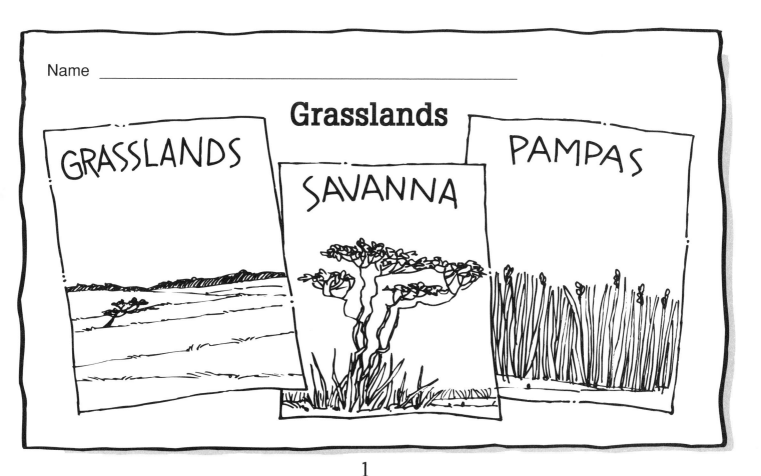

GRASSLANDS

SAVANNA

PAMPAS

Grasslands are wide areas covered with grasses. There are many kinds of grasslands around the world. They have different kinds of weather. Different kinds of plants and animals live in each one.

Grasslands may be flat or have rolling hills. Some grasslands have a few trees scattered around. The types of grasses that grow naturally depend on the amount of rainfall in the area. Today, many grasslands around the world are covered in crops planted by people.

North American Grasslands

Much of the middle of North America used to be covered in **grasslands**. There was tall grass growing everywhere. Now most of this land is being farmed. Fields of grain grow where the wild grasses used to be found.

Smaller grasslands can still be found in parts of North America.

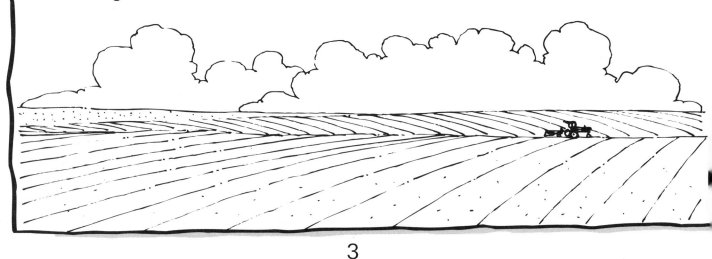

3

The Savanna

The hot grasslands of Africa are called the **savanna**. The savanna is covered in tough grasses, bushes, and a few scattered trees.

4

There are times in the year when there is very little water on these African plains. Animals have to travel far to find watering holes. At these times, animals that are usually enemies will drink from the same watering holes.

When the rains do come, the savanna turns green for a while. This is a time when there is plenty of water and food for everyone.

Pampa

The **pampa** is in South America. It has cold, dry winds that dry it out. There is very little rainfall. Only a few small trees grow among the wild grasses.

A polar habitat is very cold.

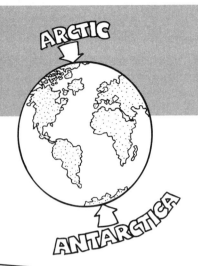

A Polar Habitat

- Make an overhead transparency of page 73.

  Ask students to tell what they already know about the polar regions. (Use questioning to draw on their prior knowledge of animals such as penguins and polar bears, weather conditions such as snow and ice, and icebergs.)

  Write student comments on a logbook page entitled "Polar Lands." Show the transparency to help them generate more information.

- Read books such as *Antarctica* by John Baines (Raintree Steck-Vaughn, 1998), *Arctic Tundra* by Donald Silver (McGraw-Hill, 1997), and *Summer Ice*: *Life along the Antarctic Peninsula* by Bruce McMillan (Houghton Mifflin, 1995), or show a video about the Arctic or Antarctica.

  Discuss what students learned from the reading or videos. Make additions or corrections to the class logbook page.

  Have students write about polar habitats for their individual logbooks, using the form on page 4.

Polar Plants

- Reproduce page 74 for each student. Read the information together, and then have students color the plants growing in the Arctic and Antarctica.

- Write a page entitled "Polar Plants" for the class logbook.

Polar Lands

It is very cold at the poles.

The land is covered with snow and ice most of the time.

Only a few kinds of animals live there.

Polar Animals

• Read appropriate parts of *Usborne World Wildlife—Polar Wildlife* by Kamini Khanduri (EDC Publishing, 1993) or *Arctic Babies* by Kathy Darling (Walker, 1996). List animals found in the polar regions in the class logbook on a page entitled "Polar Animals." (You may want to have more able students divide the animals into two groups — those found in the Arctic and those found in Antarctica.)

Write about polar animals for the class logbook.

• Use students to model how animals keep warm in the polar regions.

1. Create a "polar" area using a fan and a tub of ice. Have the fan blow over the ice to make a cold wind. (Mark off the area with masking tape to keep students safely away from the fan.)
2. Select students to dress in layers (heavy sweater, parka). Explain that many animals in cold areas have a layer of fat called blubber (sweater) covered by a layer of fur (parka) to keep warm in the bitter cold. Have students stand in the cold breeze before donning the clothing layers and again after they are bundled up. Ask them to describe the difference they feel.
3. Build a "cave" by covering a table with a heavy blanket. Set the cave in front of the cold breeze. Select students to crawl into the cave. Have them describe how they felt standing in the cold breeze outside the cave and then how they felt inside the cave.

Record the results of the activity in students' individual logbooks using the form on page 5.

Icebergs

- Read books such as *Danger—Icebergs!* by Roma Gans (Thomas Y. Crowell, 1987) and *Icebergs, Ice Caps & Glaciers* by Allan Fowler (Children's Press, 1998). Ask questions to check student recall. Work with students to write definitions of "glacier" and "iceberg" on a chart for the class logbook.

- Have students assist you in the following demonstration. Relate what happens to the ice cube to what happens to an iceberg.

You will need a clear plastic glass, an ice cube, water, and a copy of page 75 for each student.

1. Have a student place the ice cube in the glass. Ask students to predict what will happen when water is added.
2. Fill the glass entirely with water. Ask students to describe what happened to the ice. Was it what they had predicted?

   Have students observe how much of the ice is under water and how much is above water. Explain that, in the ocean, most of an iceberg is under the water just as most of the ice cube is under water.

3. Have several students try to keep the ice under water. (It will always bounce back up to the top.)
4. Use as much of this explanation of why ice floats as is appropriate for your students.

A glacier is a huge ice field moving down a mountain.

An iceberg is a hunk of ice that broke off a glacier into the sea.

Although ice is a solid, the same volume of ice will be lighter than an equal volume of water. Water molecules rearrange themselves into crystals when they freeze. The crystals take up more space with the same number of molecules. Being less dense than the surrounding water, the ice floats.

5. Reproduce page 75 and have students complete the record form for their logbooks.

Summary Activity

- Reproduce the "Polar Habitat" minibook on pages 76–79 for each student. Read and discuss the book together. Make additions or corrections to the "Polar Lands" logbook page.

- Reproduce page 80 for each student. They are to color the animals that belong in a polar habitat and cross out the animals that do not.

- Complete the "Polar" section of the Habitats chart begun on page 15.

Note: Make an overhead transparency of this page to use with page 70.

A Polar Habitat

 Habitats • EMC 859

Name _____

Polar Plants

During the summer, some of the ice melts along the edges of Antarctica. It is still very cold, but some mosses and lichens grow for a while.

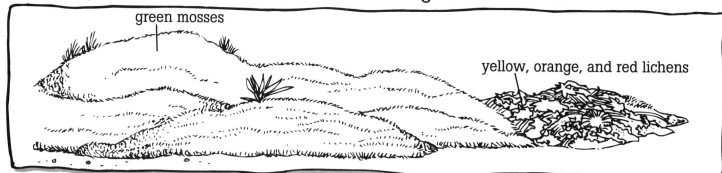

green mosses

yellow, orange, and red lichens

An arctic summer is cold and windy, but some of the ice on the **tundra** melts. Many kinds of flowering plants grow on the tundra. Mosses and lichens grow, too. Lemmings, hares, musk oxen, and caribou eat the plants.

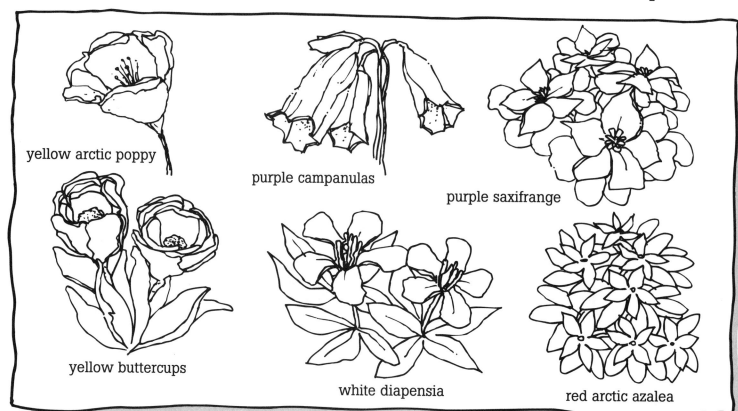

yellow arctic poppy

purple campanulas

purple saxifrange

yellow buttercups

white diapensia

red arctic azalea

Color the polar plants on this page.

Habitats • EMC 859

Note: Reproduce this page for each students to use with page 72.

Name _____

Ice and Icebergs

Show what happened to the ice cube
when water was put in the glass.

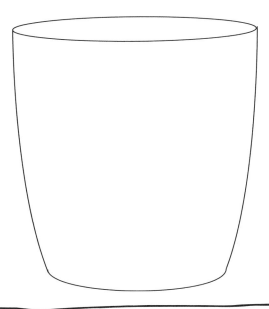

Now draw an iceberg in the ocean. Show how much of the ice is above the
water. Show how much of the ice is under the water.

75   Habitats • EMC 859

Name _____

Polar Habitats

There are two polar habitats on our planet.

ARCTIC

ANTARCTICA

1

At the North Pole you do not see much land. This is the Arctic. Most of the Arctic is a frozen ocean of ice. It is surrounded by land.

It is cold all year long. In the winter it is very, very cold. In the short spring and summer, it warms up a little. Some kinds of plants bloom.

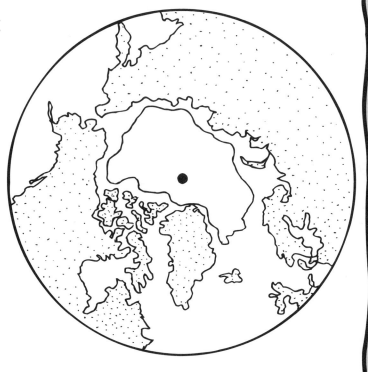

2

Many kinds of animals live in the Arctic.

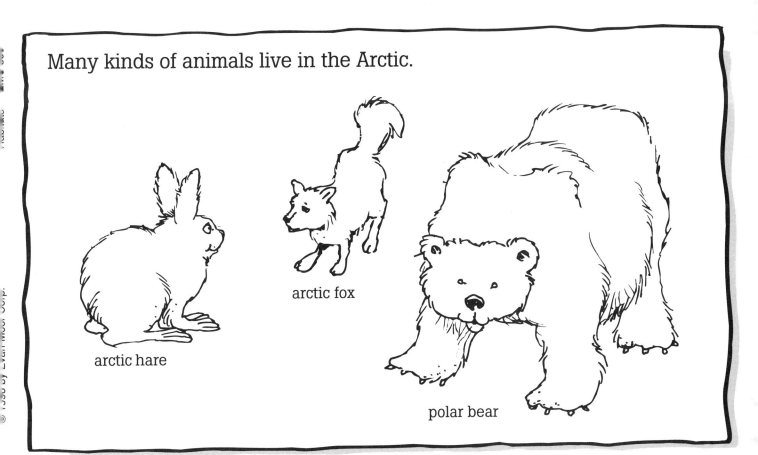

arctic fox

arctic hare

polar bear

3

Some Arctic animals change color for protection. They are brown or gray in the summer, so they can hide among the rocks. They are white in the winter, so they hide in the snow.

WINTER

SUMMER

4

There is a large continent at the South Pole. It is called Antarctica. It is a land surrounded by water. It is covered by a thick layer of ice.

Antarctica is the coldest place on Earth. It is also very windy and very dry. There are few land plants and animals living in Antarctica.

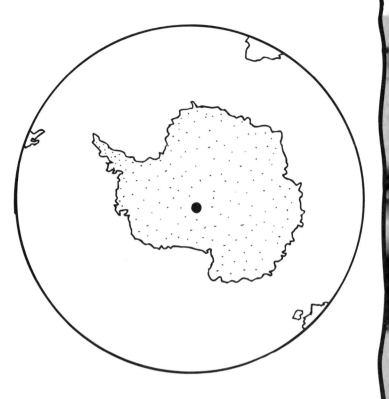

Many animals live in the ocean around Antarctica. Some of them spend time on land.

Penguins live in Antarctica. They come ashore to raise their babies.

Polar bears live in the Arctic. They give birth to their cubs in dens dug in the snow.

Note: Reproduce this page to use with page 72.

Name _____

Who Belongs Here?

Color the polar animals.
Cross out the animals that do not belong in a polar habitat.

Habitats • EMC 859